Contents

Welcome to the 30 Days Back To Me Daily Self-Care Guide and Journal!

Does this sound familiar in any way? It's Monday morning, again, and my good intentions to get up at 5 or even 6 AM are now just silent dreams passed. The alarm clock has been turned off several times and it is now 7 AM and I must force myself to get up. I throw on the most comfortable clothes I can find (that actually fit), quickly brush my teeth, throw my hair in a ponytail, maybe a little mascara (if anything), and go get everyone else ready for the day. Do the kids have sufficient lunches and snacks packed? Is there any paperwork that I need to sign & send with them? Does the homeschooled one need anything printed or supplies gathered for his lessons? I must make sure my husband has something to eat before he goes to work and, oh gosh, did I put his clothes in the dryer last night?!? Working from home, there are already work assignments piling up in my inbox. Once again, I didn't get up early enough to get my workout and shower done before the morning hustle. It's looking like it might not happen at all today, again. I get the hubby off to work, then wake the boy up to get started on his school work, then drive the high schooler to her classes, and then head back home. I walk in the door and am reminded of everything that needs to be done. I don't think I have time to fix a decent breakfast, so I grab something quick and most likely unhealthy....

Everyone's situation is a little bit different, but, after years of routines similar to this little snippet of my current daily life, many of us women- married or single, with or without children, working from home or outside the home, from all walks of life- have put OUR needs aside to care for others. We've stopped trying to find clothes that make us feel pretty and started wearing things that are just comfortable. We've stopped curling our hair and have started wearing a ponytail every day. We rarely get our hair done at a salon. Makeup? What's that?

Now, before I go any further, I need to clarify something. I think I have a pretty great life. My husband is Mr. Amazing, my children are the most incredible blessing to me (they are seriously awesome kids!), and I have a wonderful, supportive extended family. I am truly grateful for these things. But, despite how great things might be, it was becoming obvious that I needed to take some time to take better care of myself. Regardless of your situation, the same might be true for you. Because, even though we're happy to do things for others, not taking care of our own needs eventually catches up with us. We become someone we were never supposed to become. Why? Because we stopped taking care of ourselves and it meant we weren't able to do as good of a job taking care of others. If our tank was almost empty, how could we help fill theirs? One day it hit me and I realized I needed to do something about this. But how? Where would I find the time? I realized it was going to take a little while and that I would have to do it slowly. I figured out that if I do a little something for myself each day, eventually, I will find Me again. They say it takes 21 days to make a habit, but I tend to need a little more time for things to work. I figured 30 days should be a good start. So, I put together this little journal, 30 Days Back To Me, to help keep myself on track. It occured to me that I must not be the only woman going through this, so, I have decided to share it with the world hoping to help others find themselves again, too.

So often, as women, we get so caught up in taking care of everyone else's needs and wants that we tend to 'lose' ourselves. We overlook the fact that we aren't giving ourselves the attention we deserve and need in order to be able take care of others well. We forget that we are valuable and worthy of our time, too. We forget about the things we used to enjoy and become like a machine just trying to maintain.

This journal is meant to help you get back to You. It is a tool that you can use to take the time to do the things that make you feel good. It is not selfish and it may only take a few minutes a day, if you wish. But, taking care of You and remembering who You are is vital to your well being, no matter what your situation is.

Self-care is so important for improving mood, reducing anxiety, and keeping a good relationship with yourself and others. It can be difficult for self-care to come naturally. It is something that you should actively plan, rather than expect to just happen. This daily self-care guide and journal is the perfect tool to help you do just that! Each day you will choose to do a little something that YOU enjoy. There is a list of ideas included for you to try, such as giving yourself a facial, watching a sunset, taking a walk, enjoying and savoring a new treat, or even buying yourself flowers. You can also come up with your own activities that bring you joy. There are 30 journaling pages, one for each of the 30 days, where you can write down what you did and how it went. There is also space on each day's page to write 3 things you are thankful for. Gratitude is such an important part of self-care. Studies show that You can "rewire" your brain to be happy by simply recalling 3 things you're grateful for every day for 21 days.

This little journal is very simple and doesn't require too much thought. It is not filled with deep questions of time consuming self exploration and reflection. Instead, it gives you the tools to take action in finding and doing things that bring you joy. It should be fun!

As you begin, think about what the flight attendants tell you when you're on an airplane preparing for take off. They give instructions on using the oxygen masks, but make sure to tell you to put yours on first before helping anyone else. Why? Because if you are out of oxygen, there is no way you will be able to help others. Ponder that thought and enjoy the next 30 days taking care of you!

Self-care is any activity that we do intentionally in order to take care of our mental, emotional, and physical health.

Self-Care Contract

I believe that I am worth taking care of and commit to my own self-care, daily, for the next 30 days. I will not neglect my responsibilities, but, I will 'put my oxygen mask on first' so I can maintain the strength to help others.

Name:_____ Date:_____

How To Use This Journal

Each day I want you to do the following 3 things:

1. As I said earlier, gratitude plays a big role in self-care, so the first thing you will do is write down, in the space provided, 3 things that you are thankful for. Think of every little thing, every big thing, and everything in between. If you are having trouble, just do a quick search on Pinterest for 'gratitude' and you'll quickly find lots of inspiration. Don't be afraid to list even the most obvious or most mundane things. When asked how he's doing, even if things aren't going so good, my Dad will often say, "I'm breathing!". This always puts a smile on people's faces because it's so obvious, but so true, and definitely something to be grateful for!.

2. Choose an 'assignment' from the list of self-care ideas found on pages 7 & 8 and write it down in the box on the day you're on. You can even come up with your own ideas, if you'd like. The list is simply for inspiration. Take some time to complete the assignment you have chosen and think about how it makes you feel while you're doing it and once you've completed it.

3. Take a few moments to journal about your assignment. You could write something like, "This morning, I felt really crummy, but, I decided to do a random act of kindness and pay for the person's coffee in front of me. I can't believe how much of a difference it made in my day. I only hope it did the same for them." You can elaborate as much or as little as you want, just be honest with yourself. You don't even have to write full sentences. You can draw pictures, whatever you want to do. Later, you can look back on it and see what things you enjoyed most and what seemed to help you feel your best.

You can take this one step further and announce what you're doing on social media. Post your daily assignment and how it affected you in order to encourage others to take some time for themselves. Maybe they will be intrigued by what you are doing and will want to try this journal, too. I have created a Facebook group where we can all go on this journey together. If you'd like to join us, the group is called 30 Days Back To Me. It is a great place to find and give encouragement, share ideas, keep each other accountable, meet some new friends, and have some fun! I would love to meet you and hear your story, so please, consider joining us as you begin this project.

Self-Care Daily Assignment Ideas

- Write a list of things you love
- Burn a nice smelling candle
- Give yourself a pedicure
- Paint your fingernails
- Buy yourself some flowers
- Color in a coloring book
- Give yourself a facial
- Relax in the sun for 15 minutes
- Get yourself a nice shower gel/body wash and have a relaxing bubble bath or a long hot shower
- Try one of the pampering recipes from pg. 14 and use what you make
- Take a nap without feeling guilty
- Bake something
- Make a special snack (Try one of the recipes on pg. 12 or 13)
- Do something creative that you love
- Watch silly animal videos on YouTube
- Get dressed up for no reason, just because
- Buy yourself a treat and enjoy every bite
- Try something new
- Get or make a little gift for someone special
- Send a note to someone, just because
- Perform a random act of kindness
- Visit a fun new store
- Watch the sunset with your favorite evening beverage
- Watch the sunrise with your favorite morning beverage
- Get yourself a nice water bottle and use it every day
- Buy a new accessory for yourself (socks, jewelry, etc.)
- Do something different with your makeup
- Declutter a small space
- Organize a drawer or cabinet
- Take a walk outside
- Try a new coffee shop
- Buy a new coffee mug that makes you smile
- Buy some bubble gum and blow bubbles

7

- Send a happy text to someone special
- Post something positive on social media
- Listen to a podcast that interests you
- Look at pictures that inspire you (Pinterest is great for this)
- Watch your favorite movie
- Watch an episode of your favorite TV show
- Find a fun new accessory for your home (throw pillow, floral arrangement, picture, candlestick, etc.)
- Sell something online that you no longer need on Facebook Marketplace, Ebay, Craigslist, etc.
- Listen to your favorite music while cleaning (or just relaxing)
- Sit outside under the stars and dream (with your eyes open)
- Take a few minutes and write down everything that's on your mind
- Try a new hobby like crocheting, knitting, sewing, painting, etc.
- Play a favorite song from your youth
- Have a piece of your favorite fresh fruit
- Get your hair done
- Pop some bubble wrap
- Draw a picture that makes you smile
- Organize your closet
- Put together a few outfits (from your closet) that you love, including accessories
- Read something that inspires you (book, poem, magazine, online article, etc.)
- Pay something forward
- Go online and search for self-care ideas & choose one to try

Write down your own ideas here:

_____

_____

_____

_____

_____

_____

_____

Helpful Hints

In addition to your daily assignments, there are some things you can do anytime that will help you to take care of yourself. Some of these are very important necessities and others are optional. Here is a great list of ideas:

- Be Active-Do any kind of activity from lifting weights to workout videos, walking, running, dancing-whatever you enjoy. It is good to get in at least 20 minutes a day of moderate physical activity.
- Eat a well balanced diet that includes plenty of lean protein, fresh fruits & vegetables, whole grains, and healthy fats. It is best to eat whole foods versus processed foods whenever possible.
- Drink lots of water! It is recommended that adults drink eight 8-ounce glasses, which is about half a gallon. This is called the 8×8 rule and is very easy to remember. Your needs may differ, but this is a good place to start.
- Remember to take any vitamins & supplements that you or your doctor feel you need.
- Get plenty of sleep! Most adults need 7 to 8 hours of quality sleep on a consistent schedule every night. Getting enough sleep isn't only about the total hours of sleep. It is important to get good quality sleep on a regular schedule so you feel rested when you wake up.
- Get up a little earlier than everyone else and enjoy the quiet before the day begins. A great morning routine can do wonders for making the rest of your day go well. See the next page for morning routine ideas, then create your own on the following page-keep it simple!
- Have an evening routine where you get as much ready for the next day as possible. It will help you to have peace before falling asleep and make your morning go a lot smoother. See the next page for evening routine ideas, then create your own on the following page-keep it simple!
- Get yourself some nice quality comfy pajamas or loungewear that you feel comfortable in for those days when you want to relax at home.
- Have a cozy nook where you can sit and read or write in this journal and enjoy a cup of something nice to drink during your quiet time. A comfy chair with a little table and lamp is perfect.
- Laugh! Find something everyday that is funny to you, a joke book, sillly YouTube videos, etc. and LOL!

Morning Routine Ideas

- Wake Up Early
- Make your bed
- Exercise-go for a walk, workout video, stretching, etc.
- Shower or wash your face & brush your teeth
- Get dressed in something that makes you feel good & do your hair & makeup
- Write 3 things that you're thankful for in this journal
- Decide what your daily assignment will be and write it in the box on the journal page for the day
- Think about your top 3 priorities for today and write them down someplace
- Have a nice warm beverage in a mug you love
- Eat a healthy breakfast
- Take your vitamins
- Drink some water

Evening Routine Ideas

- Tidy up so you get to wake up to a nice clean space
- Set out your clothes for tomorrow
- Prepare anything you can make ahead for breakfast or lunch
- Pack anything that needs to go with you in the morning
- Glance at your schedule for tomorrow so you're prepared
- Take a moment to journal about how your self-care assignment went today, if you haven't already
- Shower/Wash your face & brush your teeth
- Put on some cozy pajamas
- Snuggle with loved ones(significant other, kids, pets, teddy bear)
- Read
- Go to bed early

☀ Morning Routine

_____
_____
_____
_____
_____
_____

Evening Routine 🌙

_____
_____
_____
_____
_____
_____

Special Snack Recipes

Chocolate Covered Strawberries

INGREDIENTS:

1 pt. Strawberries

2 c. Semisweet chocolate chips

2 tbsp. coconut oil(optional)

DIRECTIONS:

- Place a sheet of parchment paper on a large baking tray
- Rinse strawberries and pat dry
- Place chocolate chips and coconut oil in a small microwave safe bowl and microwave for 30 seconds, stir, then continue to microwave in 20 second intervals, stirring in between, until completely melted.
- Dip strawberries in chocolate and place on prepared baking sheet.
- Refrigerate for about 30 minutes or until chocolate is set.

Fruit & Cheese Kabobs

INGREDIENTS:

Strawberries, Grapes, Pineapple Chunks

Cheese

Wooden Skewers or Toothpicks

DIRECTIONS:

- Cut cheese into 1/2" square chunks
- Place a piece of fruit on the skewer then a piece of cheese and continue in an alternating pattern until the skewer is full
- Place prepared skewers on a plate and enjoy!

Squeezie Cheese & Crackers

This one is pretty self explanatory and just plain FUN... Grab your favorite crackers and a can of squeezie cheese. Create beautiful masterpieces on your crackers and chomp away!

Special Snack Recipes

Mini Snack Board

INGREDIENTS:
Crackers, Nuts, Dried Fruit, Fresh Fruit, Variety of Cheeses(Hard & Soft), Salami, Pretzels, Olives, Whatever else you like
DIRECTIONS:
Find a nice tray and arrange the items in neat little piles on the tray.

Fancy Popcorn

Pop some popcorn and add some interesting toppings. There are endless recipes online, but here are a few ideas: S'mores, Birthday Cake, Key Lime, Butter & Salt, Parmesan, Ranch.....

Fruity Sherbet Punch

INGREDIENTS:
Hawaiian Punch
Rainbow Sherbet
Lemon Lime Soda
DIRECTIONS:
Place 2 scoops of sherbet in a fun glass. Carefully pour equal parts Hawaiian Punch and soda over sherbet until glass is full. Add a fancy straw and enjoy!

Fruit Infused Water

If you get tired of plain old water, try adding fresh fruit. There are endless ideas for recipes online, but to start with, you could try blackberries & strawberries, cucumber & mint, or lemons & limes. Just clean and slice fruit and plop a few pieces in your water. Put it in a pitcher and enjoy throughout the day.

Pampering Recipes

Coconut Lime Sugar Scrub

INGREDIENTS:
1 cups white sugar
1/4 cup coconut oil
2 Tbsp fresh lime juice
Optional: zest of one lime
Optional: 3-4 drops lime essential oil

DIRECTIONS:
Mash together sugar and coconut oil until soft
and well combined. Add lime juice and zest or
lime essential oil and stir. Place in a wide
mouthed jar. To enjoy, scoop out desired amount
of scrub and use in the shower or bath for
exfoliating arms, hands, legs, and feet.

Soothing Shower Melts

INGREDIENTS:
1 cup baking soda
1/2 cup sea salt or epson salt
20-25 drops essential oils
Water (about 2-3 teaspoons)
DIRECTIONS:
In a glass bowl, pour baking soda and salt. Slowly
add water, about 2 teaspoons, and stir well. Add
just enough water so that you can squeeze the
mixture together and it holds slightly. Do not over
wet. Add 15-20 drops of essential oils of your choice
and stir well. Pour into silicone molds and press
the mixture in hard. Make sure there are no air
bubbles and it is packed tight. Let the mixture
completely dry for about 48 hours. Pop the essential
oil shower melts out of the mold and
store in an airtight container like a glass mason jar.

Day 1

Date:_____

TODAY'S ASSIGNMENT:

I Am Thankful For:

1._____

_____

2._____

_____

3._____

_____

Thoughts for today:

Day 2

Date:_____

TODAY'S ASSIGNMENT:

I Am Thankful For:

1._____

_____

2._____

_____

3._____

_____

Thoughts for today:

Day 3

Date:_____

TODAY'S ASSIGNMENT:

I Am Thankful For:

1._____
_____

2._____
_____

3._____
_____

Thoughts for today:

Day 4

Date:_____

TODAY'S ASSIGNMENT:

I Am Thankful For:

1._____

_____

2._____

_____

3._____

_____

Thoughts for today:

Day 5

Date:_____

TODAY'S ASSIGNMENT:

I Am Thankful For:

1._____

_____

2._____

_____

3._____

_____

Thoughts for today:

Day 6

Date:_____

TODAY'S ASSIGNMENT:

I Am Thankful For:

1._____

_____

2._____

_____

3._____

_____

Thoughts for today: _____

Day 7

Date:_____

TODAY'S ASSIGNMENT:

I Am Thankful For:

1._____
_____
2._____
_____
3._____
_____

Thoughts for today:

_____
_____
_____
_____
_____
_____
_____
_____
_____
_____
_____
_____
_____
_____
_____
_____
_____

Day 8

Date:_____

TODAY'S ASSIGNMENT:

I Am Thankful For:

1._____

_____

2._____

_____

3._____

_____

Thoughts for today:_____

Day 9

Date:_____

TODAY'S ASSIGNMENT:

I Am Thankful For:

1._____

_____

2._____

_____

3._____

_____

Thoughts for today: _____

_____

_____

_____

_____

_____

_____

_____

_____

_____

_____

_____

_____

_____

_____

_____

_____

Day 10

TODAY'S ASSIGNMENT:

I Am Thankful For:

1._____

_____

2._____

_____

3._____

_____

Thoughts for today:

Day 11

Date:_____

TODAY'S ASSIGNMENT:

I Am Thankful For:

1._____

_____

2._____

_____

3._____

_____

Thoughts for today:

Day 12

Date:_____

TODAY'S ASSIGNMENT:

I Am Thankful For:

1._____

_____

2._____

_____

3._____

_____

Thoughts for today:

Day 13

Date:_____

TODAY'S ASSIGNMENT:

I Am Thankful For:

1._____

_____

2._____

_____

3._____

_____

Thoughts for today:

Day 14

Date:_____

TODAY'S ASSIGNMENT:

I Am Thankful For:

1._____

_____

2._____

_____

3._____

_____

Thoughts for today:_____

Date:_____

TODAY'S ASSIGNMENT:

I Am Thankful For:

1._____
_____
2._____
_____
3._____
_____

Thoughts for today:

Day 16

Date:_____

TODAY'S ASSIGNMENT:

I Am Thankful For:

1._____
_____
2._____
_____
3._____
_____

Thoughts for today:

Day 17

Date:_____

TODAY'S ASSIGNMENT:

I Am Thankful For:

1._____
_____

2._____
_____

3._____
_____

Thoughts for today:

Day 18

Date:_____

TODAY'S ASSIGNMENT:

I Am Thankful For:

1._____

_____

2._____

_____

3._____

_____

Thoughts for today:

Day 19

Date:_____

TODAY'S
ASSIGNMENT:

I Am Thankful For:

1._____

_____

2._____

_____

3._____

_____

Thoughts for today:

Day 20

Date:_____

TODAY'S ASSIGNMENT:

I Am Thankful For:

1. _____

_____

2. _____

_____

3. _____

_____

Thoughts for today:

_____
_____
_____
_____
_____
_____
_____
_____
_____
_____
_____
_____
_____
_____
_____
_____
_____
_____
_____
_____

Day 21

Date:_____

TODAY'S ASSIGNMENT:

I Am Thankful For:

1._____
_____
2._____
_____
3._____
_____

Thoughts for today:

Day 22

Date:_____

TODAY'S ASSIGNMENT:

I Am Thankful For:

1._____

_____

2._____

_____

3._____

_____

Thoughts for today:

Day 23

Date:_____

TODAY'S
ASSIGNMENT:

I Am Thankful For:

1._____

_____

2._____

_____

3._____

_____

Thoughts for today:_____

_____

_____

_____

_____

_____

_____

_____

_____

_____

_____

_____

_____

_____

_____

_____

_____

_____

_____

Day 24

Date:_____

TODAY'S ASSIGNMENT:

I Am Thankful For:

1._____
_____
2._____
_____
3._____
_____

Thoughts for today:

Day 25

Date:_____

TODAY'S
ASSIGNMENT:

I Am Thankful For:

1._____
_____
2._____
_____
3._____
_____

Thoughts for today:

Day 26

Date:_____

TODAY'S ASSIGNMENT:

I Am Thankful For:

1._____
_____

2._____
_____

3._____
_____

Thoughts for today:
_____
_____
_____
_____
_____
_____
_____
_____
_____
_____
_____
_____
_____
_____
_____
_____
_____
_____
_____
_____
_____

Day 27

Date:_____

TODAY'S ASSIGNMENT:

I Am Thankful For:

1._____
_____

2._____
_____

3._____
_____

Thoughts for today:_____

Day 28

Date:_____

TODAY'S ASSIGNMENT:

I Am Thankful For:

1._____

_____

2._____

_____

3._____

_____

Thoughts for today:

Day 29

Date:_____

TODAY'S ASSIGNMENT:

I Am Thankful For:

1._____
_____

2._____
_____

3._____
_____

Thoughts for today:

Day 30

Date:_____

TODAY'S ASSIGNMENT:

I Am Thankful For:

1._____

_____

2._____

_____

3._____

_____

Thoughts for today:

Congratulations!

You did it! You took care of You for 30 Days! Hopefully you have established some good habits along the way and will continue to take care of yourself. Please, take a few moments and use this space to write down a plan for how you are going to make sure you don't forget about You:

Final Thoughts

I really hope you have enjoyed the last 30 days of intentionally taking the time to care for yourself. You are SO worth it! If you have found this fun little book to be helpful in your life, I would love it if you would share it with others. Maybe you want to grab another copy for yourself and also get some for friends or family so you can embark on this journey together. It can be lots of fun to do something like this with others. This journal is currently available on Amazon.

If you have any questions or would like to share with me how this book has helped you, please send me an email at 30daysbacktome@gmail.com. I would love to hear from you! Also, don't forget to check in with us in the 30 Days Back To Me Facebook Group! We would love to meet you and we value what you could bring to the group. We look forward to hearing about how your journey back to You is going.

Remember, put Your 'oxygen mask' on First!

Take Care :o)

Made in the USA
Coppell, TX
17 September 2021

62543015R00028